Saved
By the Telling

Saved
By the Telling

Eva Tihanyi

*For Lynn,
renegade, delightful
feminist miscreant
+ a terrific interview
subject.*

Eva Tihanyi

Thistledown Press Ltd.

Canadian Cataloguing in Publication Data

Tihanyi, Eva, 1956 -

Saved by the telling

Poems.
ISBN 1-895449-35-9

I. Title.

PS8589.I53S3 1995 C811'.54 C95-920161-0
PR9199.3.T55S3 1995

Book design by A.M. Forrie
Cover art by Martin McCarney
Set in Class Garamond
by Thistledown Press

Printed and bound in Canada
by Hignell Printing
Winnipeg, Manitoba

Thistledown Press Ltd.
633 Main Street
Saskatoon, Saskatchewan
S7H 0J8

This book has been published with the assistance of The Canada Council
and the Saskatchewan Arts Board.

This book is for all the women who live here

and to the memory of my grandmother
Elizabeth Kalán Tihanyi
September 13, 1905 – April 1, 1995
without whom
I would not have become
who I am

CONTENTS

WOMEN'S RITES

LIFE IN THE HOME LANE

WHO YOU ARE IS WHAT YOU SEE

Women's Rites

*I have always thought of a myth as something that
never was but is always happening.*

— Jean Houston, *The Possible Human*

Let's begin with Eve, how she got pigeon-holed as a rib. Instead of being hailed a hero for her daring, she got the shit knocked out of her with an apple and never recovered.

Now consider my friend, an attractive woman with guts and gusto. Slotted at 17 by an accidental pregnancy, she lacks money, purpose, self-respect. You might say she got her life knocked out of her by an older man with tight jeans and a black Corvette. She's now 36.

There are other stories worth reconsidering. For instance, I'm convinced that Persephone dropped willingly down to Hades, happy to get away from her mother for part of the year. She didn't admit this to anyone, of course (neither did my friend when she first sank into that bucket seat), having learned already the value of reticence as self-defence.

Persephone got on well in the Underworld, knew when to keep her mouth shut — or open, depending on Hades' pleasure. She had streetsmarts, that woman, as does my friend. No one gives either enough credit. But at least Persephone ended up with the best of two worlds. Not so my friend. The guy with the 'Vette has been in jail for years; her mother phones regularly, still inquires why her daughter doesn't give "that nice man" a chance; and every night she dreams of apples.

We're sitting over coffee one evening, my friend, husband and I, when her boyfriend phones demanding to know where she's been all day. When she tells him she won't answer to anyone, he slams the phone down, screeches five minutes later into her driveway. He doesn't wait for an invitation, rams right in.

He yells, she yells back, they have it out. My husband and I remain silent, are sudden statues, backdrops to the argument — though the men, I sense, are ready. Attack, defend. Two sides of the same male hand, women at its mercy. Always.

Before a woman dares open her mouth to a man, she'd better learn alternatives to words. Inevitable that he'll want to shut her up, one way or another. But she'll keep on saying anyway, in other ways. Will be forced to remember Philomela's pain transferred onto tapestry: art fueled by the absolute need to tell.

You see him stop for a moment

It might be over, you hope it's over,
but then he comes at her in the bathroom,
they are both naked, they should be making love
but instead, in a parody of childhood games,
he smashes her with a pillow,
shoves her against a wall

And then she's down
cowering beside the toilet, her hands
raised to protect her face, whimpering
Don't hurt me, don't hurt me
as if the words
could ward off evil, call off
the mad dog in him —

What happens next
depends on how much faith you have
in words

Imagine that a man hands you a sheet of paper, says choose which you believe. On one side is written: *The statement on the other side of this paper is false.* And on the reverse: *The statement on the other side of this paper is true.*

You feel confused, of course, know very well you can't possibly win at this. With either choice, you're back to where you started: unable to choose. A kind of verbal Escher, like the hand drawing the hand. Or the old adage about the rock and the hard place.

You pour yourself a glass of wine, sit back, study the paper, the man who gave it to you. You would like to shake this man, this sly giver of paper. You are embarrassed by yourself, the way you continue sitting with him at the same table in the same house, your head cocked in fashionable bewilderment, shoulders slumping. You should be searching for a solution, at the very least countering with your own sheet: blank on both sides, stunningly silent.

But no: it's easier to gamble than to will. You bet he'll eventually grow tired of the game, take the paper from your hand, set his lighter to it. And all will be well not because you chose to end it well, but because it ended.

My neighbour's husband comes home late on a Saturday night, announces he no longer loves her, is leaving. She sits down, has to, cannot suddenly think of a single thing to say. Eleven years, two kids, one mortgage later, he's leaving. His choice, her fate.

The next morning, as she goes from room to room changing other people's beds at the Journey's End, she wishes she could tidy her own life so quickly, efficiently — pull off the soiled sheets, replace them with fresh ones, white and crisp.

He swills
nine cans of beer between 10 and 4
because he's bored, pissed off
at The Wife
who's out of commission with the flu

Too bad she has to take it lying down,
the way he stands over her, lording
his disgust

She thinks of how it would feel
to throw up on his shoes,
not have to clean it up

In memory of Bronwen Wallace

This started as a simple poem for Naomi Wolf,
you know, the kind Bronwen wrote Virginia, the kind
women write to women they admire

I, too, wanted this simple, wanted
to forget about the hair in the sink,
the pervasive stench of cat shit

Didn't want to think about the laundry
or the bills or my son's sore throat

Wanted to talk about how much had changed,
how we had traded victimhood for power

I wanted with all my heart
to see the wine glass half full
instead of half empty

But somehow I kept coming back to them,
the small details that suck us down like quicksand,
the daily mud we battle through

Kept remembering my neighbour,
house for sale, telling me about her husband

Couldn't get her voice out of my mind,
a voice explaining fear, the impossibility
of arguing with a fist

I kept coming back to it,
this corrupt version of progress:
a woman's place no longer in the home
because she isn't
safe in it

Picasso's woman irons,
gravity incarnate, pressing her weight
against cloth, against
the creases of living

He painted her when he was a young man
in Paris in the spring

She too is young,
still able to infuse domestic chores
with a certain postural poetry;
still able
at the farthest edges of her naïveté
to imagine Picasso
ironing

This is how he first sees her: she's sitting with friends at her favorite café, throwing her wit around, a tense weight. She places her left hand, fingers fanned, on the wooden table. Drives a knife between her spread fingers, moves methodically to each new space. Time after time the blade thunks down, often grazing flesh, until blood blooms across the pink roses on her black lace glove. She continues, not out of boredom or insolence but need. She would like to photograph this if she could, his eyes as dark as hers, skewered to the scene by an invisible knife.

Olé! she cries, both matador and bull, victor and sacrifice.

I knew a man once who, after his girlfriend broke off with him, lined his palm with razor cuts and pressed it along the dormitory walls, an adult Hansel leaving blood instead of crumbs. He wanted to make sure someone found him, led him out.

Too bad the man who went to him was a descendant of the Minotaur, a prisoner of his own maze, monstrous. He didn't bother blaming the girlfriend, was impressed by the bleeding hand, considered it a sign of seriousness. *No art without suffering*, he said, and Hansel believed.

So they became partners in a private labyrinth, one heart-broken, the other enjoying the sanguine mood, encouraging it for Hansel's sake.

I picture them still: side by side on the bed, watching with utmost seriousness the serious blood.

The singsong conviction she chomps at like a bit,
cannot swallow or discard:

> *He's taking the woman to the slaughterhouse,*
> *slaughterhouse, the slaughterhouse*

She's 50, maybe 55,
sitting on the streetcar
on a fine June day,
her mind locked in the world
but never wholly of it,
purgatory

> *He's taking the woman to the slaughterhouse,*
> *slaughterhouse, the slaughterhouse*

She recites her refrain
as if it were a nursery rhyme
while the embarrassed passengers stare,
try not to, think
of explanations that might fit her,
this pink-clad aberration
who knows it is night in God's head
and can't forgive him for it

I'm talking about literature
to a group of alcoholic women

I read them poems, feel
their round cynical eyes
assess my clothes, face,
fingernails

Is that a perm?
one of them ventures
after my five-minute oration
on the value of language

Pompous bitch
they must be thinking
Who is she to tell us?

I haven't smoked in years,
light my fourth cigarette;
am a swimmer
who suddenly finds herself
too far out to sea
and flounders

I am a foreign element
in their amnesic waters,
a strange gut disturbance

Perhaps in a day, a year,
one of them will spit me out
in words

BREAKTHROUGH

After reading the journals of Sylvia Plath

You once thought of him as a fawn
but he turned satyr;
horns rose from his head
and he gouged your heart with them,
bucked you to the wall

Now, in his absence,
you fill your heart
with a violent cacophony,
vow to give it form

It will be a tryst
between you and the words,
the final love affair;
you will press yourself into paper,
your blood will be the watermark

The night stares at your hand
through the window, moves closer,
a black fox

You have gathered yourself
together for this;
you have been waiting, building
all your life this complex sepulchre,
this hymn for your heart's
last
mad-muscle dancing;
and as the blood
ascends to its flowering,
you throw your fist into the page

      which sings at last as you willed it:
      a bludgeoning thunder
      echoing in frozen snow

He really loves you, he told me
he worships you from afar,
that's what he said — worship —
and don't give me this shit
about your being married,
that's not the point,
deep down you want him
to carry you off, ravage you —
smirk all you want
but I was young once
and far more beautiful
and men came knocking at my door,
men I didn't think were good enough —
don't make the same mistake,
I'm telling you
I'm really a primitive at heart,
just imagine being carried off like that,
it's the children of the strongest
you want to have,
it's the strongest you want,
believe me

People say she's hyper, well they don't know the half of it, what goes on inside her head and for starters what does hyper mean, there's no such word. It's doubtful that hyper would describe it anyway, it's more like rain falling upward, her life is like that too but that's another story, at the moment we're talking about the contents of a head, a myriad of things and they all move at once sometimes which of course is bound to cause collisions. Because nothing's perfect, not even thoughts in the head — least of all thoughts in the head — so she ends up thinking about things even when she doesn't want to, thought happens despite all effort, and sometimes it's interesting and sometimes it's not and sometimes it makes her hyper but being hyper (people say) won't help distinguish which is which. In fact people say she shouldn't think because she's dangerous then, which is what it all comes down to in the end, doesn't it, danger and the fear of it.

for Dianne

Years ago, when we happened upon
that shelf of glass heads in a Yonge Street store,
I had a flash of recognition, knew such a head
would be the perfect gift from a woman to a man:
see-through, smooth and breakable

You agreed, and we each
bought one for our husbands
so they could watch what they imagined
were our dreams

*Not unlike the fishbowl concept we remarked
or perhaps a miniature shop window;
it might keep them out of trouble,
would certainly keep the focus
off our real heads, the subversive ones
with their thick tangle of hair
and female synapses*

We thought of it as simply
heading off trouble

And our husbands, both avid collectors
of unusual gifts, were grateful recipients;
spent many an hour staring through the glass

Odd though, isn't it, how you and I
have carried the glass head, its image,
with us all these years;
have admired its green hue,
its weird opaque transparency;
have felt compelled
to re-imagine it in words:
ours,
or theirs?

Last week, in an old newspaper yellowing in my desk drawer, I came across this item:

Princess Anne hates to sign autographs, but it was front page news in Britain yesterday when the princess made an exception signing a get well card — for a horse! The lucky horse, Peter The Great, injured in a road accident recently, is convalescing. . . .

Maybe it's just a matter of too much time spent with horses instead of humans. Maybe the card was simply a frivolous gesture, a comic lapse in the royal brain. Or possibly something more sinister, Freudian — a hint that Anne is susceptible to equine charm, and is secretly writing a book titled *The Erotic Equestrian Experience*.

Perhaps people just don't give her enough credit. Perhaps hers is a noble love, a passion for the true horse: galloping beast of instinct and desire, fleet-footed carrier of warriors and Muses, harbinger of magic across otherwise empty plains.

for Dianne, Darlene, Ricki and Kim

1

Why we five have gathered here:

To celebrate the circle

To be, for a time,
seeds of the same apple

2

We read the runes,
recognize importance,
drink from blue goblets
the colour of healing

It is the apple season,
the time of completion

We see what we believe,
and believing is seeing

3

A round-table lunch overlooking the vineyards and then the drive
home, all of us giddy and exuberant and abundantly daring. Which
is why I'm in the mood to pick apples, jump out eagerly as soon as we
roll to a stop by the orchard. Why, grinning like some latter-day Eve
on freshly released endorphins, I ignore the NO TRESPASSING sign,
pull five apples from the bountiful branches. No snake in sight, no
Adam either. Just Eve and her friends, a party, apples for all.

It has to happen though, it is inevitable, the black car that brakes to a halt as Eve, apple-laden, runs across the road. God has arrived, perfectly punctual, just as nasty and humourless as always. "Can't you read?" he says, belligerence his obvious strong suit. Eve is promptly accused of theft, and payment is demanded. He wants a dollar, she gives him two, and the matter is settled, God (as usual) getting twice as much as he expected.

4

It is the fall equinox,
the day of half light and half darkness

We sit in the kitchen around the pine table,
five women sculpting goddesses, goddesses sculpting,
while the apple-scented candle burns
and the harvest wine sweetens our tongues,
warms our fingers as they work the clay

Wonders are forming, evolving
in the urgent silence of our shaping hands

As the sun travels south
across the celestial equator,
so too we head down into heat,
the gut energy of creation

What we make is who we are
in the making

5

Sunday morning, a final pilgrimage,
five pairs of heels
clicking along the hospital hallway

We bring our grandmother an apple

It is an offering, fruit of our hunt,
taste of our triumph

But it is she who gives us the greater gift,
the last words in our communal journal:

> *Love one another*
> *Trust in one another*
> *Do not forget me*

Wholeness, closure,
the Goddess's immortal heart;
a blessing

Life in the Home Lane

In the hospital room,
an efficient, electric quiet:
the hum of clocks, lights, furnaces,
all mechanisms working

It is November and raining,
a myriad grays window-framed

Amid the odour of uneaten meals and urine,
an old woman lies, softly breathing

Through no fault of her own
she is not who she is

Not the woman you know,
have always known: strong,
brimming with will

Her inertness betrays her: impostor

And it changes you, the terrible knowledge,
when you recognize yourself in her, discover
the ending which belongs to both of you;
admit, finally,
that breathing is not living,
no

My mother bleaches her hair
in a one-room flat
while her Danish Modern furniture
rots in her landlord's garage

She is cracked like a mosaic
left too long in the fire,
hers a decade of piecing
parts into the whole,
the whole into its parts

And through the long slide down the years
no one knew, will ever know
my mother's dreams of cold, of snow

My father, graying at the temples,
is thinner than he used to be;
his hands with their immaculate nails
rest in his lap like sleeping children

He is worn as a slipper
and shaped to a second wife's foot,
his a decade of shuffling
over thick suburban carpet
in over-heated rooms

And through this stifled blaze of years
how he ached for cold, for snow
no one ever knew, will know

As another year of silence
falls from the calendar,
I imagine her exploring malls,
reading cheap romances, staring
for hours at air, photo albums,
the drafting degree
beside the welfare cheque;
imagine her taut gaiety
braced for breaking,
her body fat with boredom
massed in front of me,
obstacle, reminder

Ten years since he left
yet love for my father
still ticks in her heart
like a perfect clock,
timeless

I imagine peeling
the decade from her face,
finding her as she was
and somehow understanding

You wondered how it happened to your mother;
now you're finding out

It starts with the way the table
suddenly taunts you with its massive wooden insolence
and you realize you've grown separate,
breathing through the days like a wingless moth
still and silent
save for a heart tolling
against stillness and silence

It continues when in the bath
you notice your winter-pale thighs, unsightly logs,
heavy beneath the water, your whole body
nothing but weight, mass,
the solidity that keeps you here
working backwards from death:
the point of departure, the given

But it is the ride to work that truly frightens you,
the way you find yourself
laughing along with the woman at the back of the bus
for no reason, every reason, laughing
like your mother the day her divorce
arrived in the mail: laughing

We drive to work, you behind the wheel,
and on this June morning
when the beast in animals flourishes
it is the dead one on the road I feel for —
decapitated, mangled —
the one you coast over
without flinching

I think of my father,
his unbridled temper
trampling whatever crossed it,
how as a child
I stared out past him
through window to sky, to clouds rolling,
white tumbleweed on blue prairie,
and learned with each moment
new survival in metaphor and analogy

> so that now
> when you say *have a good day*
> as I leave the car,
> I can answer *you too*
> without flinching

At six months
you tossed me into my grandmother's arms
like a basketball to the nearest teammate,
then ran from the court

The two of you — my mother, my father —
in your hopeful daring twenties
haycarting across the Hungarian border
in the January night

Too much risk with an infant
you thought, and we all survived

Six years later
you collected me at the airport,
a long-lost suitcase, contents
not remembered

What you found was, in your view,
mouthy, clumsy, undignified;
a child in need of lessons

And so you forced me to the top bunk
to cure my fear of heights,
cut my hair short enough
to ensure it could no longer hold
my grandmother's ribbons
(you said I needed style)

I was not like my four-year-old brother,
by birth an instant North American kid
to match the Campbell's soup,
the chrome and plastic furniture

What I was you did not want —
a small self
flying open-souled and curious
to her faraway fairytale parents
who now expect
all they could not give

They say:

> It's important to discuss procedures —
> shave, enema, intravenous, epidural,
> breastfeeding, possible Caesarean
>
> Don't let yourself be bullied
>
> Know what you want
>
> Be firm

They say:

> Eat well, get exercise, prepare
>
> Learn how to rest, breathe, control
> the body's involuntary whims
>
> Be ready

What they don't say:

> When finally you hold him, head
> still blood-crusted, hands
> smallest starfish on your belly,
> the pain over, just beginning,
> there is a love beyond love

Know this

1

The window frames a blue pause
in the run of winter:
clear sky, the snow
embossed with faint outlines
(buried branches, rock tips)

Before your eyes, falling:
the domino line of centuries,
time sweeping backward
to the antediluvean world,
the cave in winter

Here, under your blanket
of tumultuous hair,
you are animal, and woman,
urge incarnate

The child who gasps first breath
between your thighs
is unnamed and ageless,
body of your body

Already, death blooms within him,
certain flower

Safety
is not knowing this

2

When you return from the edge of yourself
to your own time,
the warm woodglow of the sideboard,
the cats dreaming cat dreams,
your son, five months old,
is cooing his marvel at the plastic rabbit
in his hands

This is the familiar life,
the comfortable evolution

The lines around your eyes
grow stealthily more pronounced,
your hair grays

The days are more and more a recognition
of these and other things, all carefully sounded
like the child's proud verbal pointing:
apple   bubble   face

Names occupy the world
with the assurance of buddhas,
meaningful and placid,
each a soothing roundness
complete in itself,
each word a hologram, in each
the world recreated

You summon it now, your son's name,
that small melody

Brendan, you say,
and know that in the saying of a name
is born the first danger

Submit
to the truth that you are

To the you that is true
submit

Be of the now, the was, and the will

Be the question,
then answer it

You gaze upward, point out cloud shapes
to the small boy who holds your hand

He, meanwhile, looks up at you,
the man who knows the sky,
can lift him toward it

I step into the background,
grant myself space, a new perspective;
permit myself
to see you as you are,
the person, not the man,
whose gift of self I returned,
unrequited

The one I have hurt
who now says he is leaving,
too late for my recognition of patterns,
the whole picture

It would be easy now
to do as I have always done,
see anger only

Instead
I see the child's face, his certainty
that you will not drop him

I did not have such faith

It would be easier
to galvanize the heart toward hatred
or wrench it tightly shut
or tranquilize it into silence;
easier to pretend I don't care

This is honesty:
permitting the heart to feel,
no matter how great the consequence,
how much the pain

Who You Are is What You See

1

Imagine
being
imagined

2

We re-invent what we already know,
imagine unicorns
because we've seen horses and horns

Beneath the headline:
a picture of Tevfik Esenc,
face deeply furrowed as plowed land
but jovial above the suit and tie
donned for the photographer

There was a time
in the Caucasus valleys
when 50,000 spoke Oubykh

Now there is one:
Tevfik Esenc, Turkish farmer

On his tongue alone
the 82 consonants, 3 vowels,
of this sound symphony;
and when he dies
yet another silence will gap a world
gouged already with extinctions

Here, too, languages dying with farmers:
the beaten fields fading
and in them, the weathered cry
of failing barns

Losing: the vernacular
of clean distance, cattle brawn and wheat sway

Eventually, headline and picture:
the last Canadian farmer
speaking farm

It was one of those days, quiet and dreary,
the ones perfect for neglected errands,
chores of the heart

I had been putting it off for months,
the laundering of my self-esteem
heaped at the bottom of my bedroom closet

It was in good company, mind you,
with shoes and boxes of Kleenex
and assorted old clothes I somehow
never seemed to get around to bagging

So I gathered my self-esteem
(there was more of it than I remembered)
and, because handwashing was not my style,
carried it to the machine, which I set
on *cold water* and *delicate*,
a contradiction of method, I thought,
but necessary

Imagine my surprise when the cycle ended
and there was my self-esteem, shrunken
to half its size, huddled like a wet waif
around the agitator

So now the problem was
how to return my self-esteem
to a wearable size

It wasn't till later that night
I came across it in a magazine:
an ad for ESTEEM CLEANERS

For the tough job you can't handle, it said

Esteem expansion guaranteed

It was the answer I'd been waiting for

I would drop off my self-esteem,
pick it up the next day, clean
and freshly pressed, miraculously re-inflated

No mess, no fuss,
and I would once again
have my prized garment, ready
for whatever would be spilled upon it

Think of how we groaned
through Restoration Literature,
shared our mock suffering over after-class beer
while the days flickered by
unsteady as old movies

In the pub window
our blurred reflections wavered, you
with husband and children and suburban predicaments
talked of balance
while I, a bold eighteen, quoted poetry
I hadn't yet lived

Life for me was certain then,
a love/hate proposition,
choices arrow-straight, flat as line drawings

The hundred shades of gray you spoke of
I didn't dare imagine

And it's taken me years to learn
that balance is a sphere,
not scales

1

At dinner you say nothing,
yawn, look tired,
your silence an aggression
I defend against

When conversation does burst from you
it is in sporadic volleys, word explosions

After midnight, in the hotel room
we're like girls in a dorm
drinking Cokes, swapping stories

You say you're tired of smiling
at the wrong people at the right time

You say people wear you out

What you don't say:

> that there's a toughness about you,
> an arctic resilience
> like that of the lichen or the dwarf pine,
> and you like your eyes open
> no matter what the landscape
> or the weather

2

We progress to next day's lunch

You spoon your way through soup,
talk about death and displacement
in their personal forms

These are not elegant stories

They have the force of a heart
stopping on a strange street

The most you can do is tell me;
the most I can do is listen

3

After lunch, you take photographs:

> a barbershop, the barber
> shaving his own face,
> embarrassed though laughing
> as you aim the camera;
> he jumps behind a partition,
> refuses

You are like the barber:

> you laugh and keep moving,
> do not surrender,
> not even to poetry perhaps

There is always the mythic train to catch,
northbound

> except your train
> moves on solid tracks,
> and it's no myth
> that between taiga and tundra
> stubborn trees survive

1

High in the Cambrian Mountains
the sheep stand, statue-still
in the slate distances

As we watch them
we are forming into history,
the outlines of our changing selves
layered, traceable as fossils

Of course we know nothing of this

Nor of how we will open and close
quickly as apertures,
retain everything, accommodate
whole mountains, every nuance of light
upon their peaks

2

We return home, to another continent

The camera is packed away,
the sun closeted

She sits in her red rocking chair
fueling her thoughts with gin,
shrinking down the night

I am witness to her fear
and to her love, both large
and inadmissable

She knows this,
speaks only of the dark heavens
so much smaller and safer in comparison

Yet she moves to the window, dares
to take in the moon

For months
every shape the moon holds
she holds also, in her
something embrace-shaped and miraculous,
a female universe she carries in her
like a talisman

Even after she expels the lunar magic,
it continues to light her,
feather across her shoulders
like a gossamer shawl

3

Now, years later,
as I stare from the car window
at the empty gravel rectangle
where the house once stood, the house
where we exchanged beginnings
to take with us, grow on,
I can't help but remember
how the sun bowed down, a windfall light
among the sadly splendid ruins,
while two women, *in the sun
that is young once only,* were young too
for a first and final time

Later I'll want to deny it,
how at this moment
I want to travel her hair's bright distance,
sunlit road along her back

All private evolutions grow from this,
the admitting and the not admitting,
a struggle always
between yes and no, an equal fear
of checking the moment,
not checking it

a variation on *The Anniversary* by Magritte

It happened when she was young,
when there were things she wanted to know,
edges she wanted to walk along with words,
longings she curved into

She planned to leave home, he wanted to marry her:
two ideas amiably complected—or so it seemed

Then she started seeing things:

> the books piled, unread, on her dresser;
> the dances hidden in her bedside radio;
> the green outside withering into brown;
> everything losing lustre

He did not notice
that her face turned slowly into stone, grew
until it filled the frame of his vision

She wrote letters to herself, spent hours
thinking of words with which to think;
then she began to say
and the saying changed her

She told him she wanted
the world windowing open around her,
the wild lemon sun squeezing itself in

She told him dreams of white stucco villas
on the tips of Greek islands,
high-ceilinged brownstones on old Parisian streets

He spoke of rings and calendars
as her face turned suddenly light,
lifted skyward, away from him

Not England, ever;
Greece maybe, or Spain — hot countries
where passion flourishes like the sun,
fans out exultant as a peacock's tail

Occasionally of others
but that's mostly for revenge

And when I'm serious,
of Kafka, how the body moving against mine
might be transformed by morning
into a controversial insect

What I think of when I make love to a man
is not necessarily what I want to think of;
in fact, it would be preferable not to think at all,
the not-thinking an erotic white noise
to fill the space between breaths

Lately though
my thoughts have taken a different turn:
there is a suitcase on the bed,
and I'm packing the vital signs, including
the heartbeat, the silence after it

Your voice compels me

I lust after it,
dream of it singing into me,
ingenuous, erotic

Picture you, phone in hand,
faithful to fate, whatever role
it has assigned you

I think of it often, its inflections,
the way it catches on certain words,
imbues them with importance,
an irrational necessity

When you say *Oh God, oh God*
you mean so much to me
invoking the Almighty
like some private punctuation,
I believe

In your voice I hear you,
and I invent
directions into your life

And I ache

The two of them
in a white convertible,
sweeping through time

Unresisting road,
turquoise summer light

She glances
at the face beside her,
finds that she herself
is being watched

No true vocabulary
for that gaze,
so flame-blue and perfect,
nor for her longing
to burn in it

It seems that whenever we meet, life's a story. Today no exception, as we sit, beer bleary, in the bar where years ago you first faced your lost sister. You haven't seen her since, have come through this town only when necessary, one eye cocked backward, anticipating the inevitable.

It is late afternoon and raining, the room dark with barlight, the stale, smoky air dismal with September. A world of the interior, necessary.

I wonder which house she lives in. Should I ask him? you say, as you nod toward the bartender. He is suspicious but forthcoming. Yes, he knew her. No, she's no longer here, went back — years ago — across the sea. You are relieved and disappointed, the paradox of wishes granted.

And suddenly you are crying, you are who you are, you won't be back.

Think of dusk
folding into the horizon, the day
gradually collapsing, sky and earth
pressed together, sealing us in

Or think perhaps of a salad dressing
in which oil and vinegar have separated
forming two distinct layers
and a demarcation line
which, when the bottle is shaken,
vanishes

We're always on a border,
and borders change and vanish at whim

It's simply a matter
of who does the pressing and shaking,
and when

There's warmth in October,
a peculiar burnished light
that gilds trees, buildings, roads
with the glow of ancient trumpets

In this light
the world is eternally possible,
the opening and closing of distances
simply a matter of time

Mere days ago
you said you could picture
exactly how the airport would look,
afternoon sun falling through windows,
milling bodies
waiting for the boarding call

You, too, are familiar
with the myriad locations of goodbye,
the countless individual histories
reborn in these gestures:
hug, lifting of suitcase, final wave

The escalator takes me up,
light already shifted

You wait, coffee in hand,
coat open, backlit as a photograph

          and I see you still
          because vision persists
          though reality moves

You walk along the urban sidewalk,
feel again
the red rush of autumn,
the rioting sad heart
undiminished in the seed of things,
the chill in your spine
coursing down in long tingles

And as you feel this,
already it is ending

The curbside puddles harden in the wind,
autumn yielding to albino trees,
white sculpture in blue light

As you move into the cold season
your blood for an instant pauses,
recognizes something
you've grown to hold inside you,
small
but warm as fur

Late afternoon on the Sunday road,
the small towns closed, ambiguous,
in the muted November countryside

Immersed in lukewarm moods
and medial observations, we drive on
deeper into evening, colder weather,
until even our small talk
shrinks to silence

The inner landscape is more fluent,
less prone to freezing at low temperatures

It stretches on, unperturbed
by the circular horizon we leave,
move toward; the successive moments
we pass through but never inhabit

It is what makes us possible,
why, at the motel,
your boots leaning against mine
beside the dresser,
I am able to offer you a different submersion:

> heat like a benthal cold,
> searing through you like mint

Outside, the sky expands and contracts
like a great slow heart,
the windows around us, dark screens
on which potentials
cock their heads like deer,
pause

We linger over last drinks,
complain of the times we are ordinary
in an ordinary world

      and the raw eclectic life,
      domesticated, well-done to boredom,
      petrifies: hard
      to suck ecstasy from a stone

And though season after season
a wild hope guides us
to books, friends, foreign lands,
in both of us
a fear breathes, deeply
like a hunger:

      that years from now
      (our bodies no longer strong
      or fashionable, demanded
      or demanding) only our eyes
      will hint at what we are tonight:

young, charged with a peculiar beauty,
speaking of the cordons
through which our possible selves glide,
composed and sunlit, undulating
towards the sea

We started by talking about lovers,
the can't-live-with-or-without-them scenes,
the irresistible lure of sex

By the third drink we were into families,
their blatant omnipotence,
haunting contradictions

We told of our mothers, yours
dead when you were twelve, mine
out of touch for years,
how they lived on in us
like persistent fairytale queens
necessary to the story

They were easy,
these exchanges of our selves,
motherless, yearning;
and I've since pictured you often, like me
bent over your sleeping children
as they dream their hags and witches,
sheep in wolves' clothing

Sometimes they smile,
and we know that in those dreams
we are kind and soft-voiced,
the givers of music

I'm thinking of you again tonight,
imagine that provinces away
you're walking along the South Saskatchewan River
looking up, as I am,
at our shared moonlight
while our mothers speak in us
(uncanny ventriloquism),
their young selves almost audible,
singing

Around you, in rooms everywhere,
year-end rituals deflate into sleep

So predictable, these anemic celebrations,
one year metamorphosing into the next

You aren't in a good mood,
think of impostures, impostors,
poses of all kinds, read
Tarot cards for your friends,
wondering all the while
about your own fate,
impending losses

The beer stales in your throat
as suddenly you feel it:
imponderable Time,
exultantly menacing,
surrounds you, breathes you in

A 1920s ice cream parlour
with arborite tables, oak booths
layered with graffiti

Two women pick at french fries,
order another round of rye;
for once, the ice cream doesn't tempt them

One has just come from the doctor,
talks of an abnormal Pap smear,
the word *dysplasia*

Displaced

That is how she feels suddenly;
removed from her own future,
which she has always taken for granted

A future that now seems
unavoidably stoppable

They both stare at the names
carved into the wall beside them,
each name a proclamation:
I was here, I counted

What neither can say:
No matter what happens,
will you remember me

Outside your window, snow

What you see:
a herd of white horses sleeping

This, a quirk of faith:
that God is the eye you trust —
your own,
as it smooths a mane
in the quickening sunlight

It is always February,
wind attacking branches, toppling
the snow from them,
coup after small coup

The heart is weather bent;
sways onward, a lost ship
ricocheting among the ice floes;
dreams of Van Gogh's ochre fields
where sunlight always happens

If happiness is sanity,
the heart vows to be happy

Combustible, stoked with joy,
it eagers skyward, longs
to be yanked into a high place
with the sun

But the body,
both prison and prisoner,
binds, is bound

Sanity, sanity hums the frustrated heart
as it dreams its balustrade of light,
the slide upward;
imagines itself, finally,
lifted free

Today she's flying to Greece, dreads
the long flight, the act
of getting there;
would prefer to simply blink herself
into the turtle days, slow and heavy,
lazing along forever

She dreams of continuous summer,
a blue and yellow set, her true self
waiting in the wings,
patient understudy, silent playwright

She recognizes this woman,
sunlit, merging with the water,
with others
who've arrived also at the apex:
mind and body old enough, young enough,
not to be enemies

The dream grows:
she paints the scenes,
wills herself into them,
articulates the rhythms of her life,
wave after wave, shoring;
begins to unlearn her masks,
become the play itself

At home
her friends speak well of her unfolding,
think all the while of height,
a night plane
airborne into breathlessness,
the long flight
getting there

Manuel, man of *mañana*,
bounces his yellow taxi
along the old stone streets
as we, his boisterous passengers,
shout *Musica! Musica!*,
urge him to crank up the radio

He thinks we've had too much tequila,
isn't used to such glee from the tourists
but obliges, all of us grinning happily,
you and I in the back seat clapping,
fitting the moment
like two hands in a perfect pair of gloves

Arriba! cries Manuel, *Andale!*
his Spanish exhortations
potent as spells, the cab now cruising
along the smoother pavement of the The Malecon,
pushing across the city
in the sultry night

We have faith that surely
anything might happen,
that as the cumbia rhythm engages our blood
and our laughter lifts through the open windows,
nothing matters but this:

        the power and the feeling,
        the renegade hearts
        in the fools who are us

You step into happiness eagerly
as if it were a scalding bath in winter,
welcome and luxurious

The days pass on,
smooth as water, elusive as mercury,
wearing away your necessary edges,
washing over you in steady currents
as you lie motionless
in a fabulous absence of pain

You are speechless,
though a question mark
curls like a serpent
in your apple-scented throat,
winds gradually
into your silent core;
but the warmth lulls you
and you do not move

It is easy, this immersion,
like drowning

It is only your hand that can save you,
your hand which happiness cannot alter,
which reaches out into the shock of air
and listens,
poised to record
on a seemingly empty page